M000289681

BE STILL

www.marilynrandolph.com

Marilyn M. Randolph

2019
Amari Rise Publishing
3315 San Felipe Rd #97 San Jose Ca 95135
www.MarilynRandolph.com

2016
Copyright © 2016
by Marilyn M. Randolph

For information address: Amari Rise Publishing. 3315 San Felipe Rd #97, San Jose, CA 95135

Marilyn Randolph *BE STILL*

Printed in the United States of America

ISBN: 978-0-9916231-8-1 (Softcover) ISBN: (eBook)

Publisher – Amari Rise Publishing.

Cover Design – Madison McClintock www.madisonjmcclintock.com

and BookClaw

Editing – Crystal City and Amari Rise Editing Team

Printed in the United States of America

Short extracts may be used for review purposes.

Unless otherwise indicated, Bible quotations are taken from The King James Version.

Scriptures marked KJV are taken from the KING JAMES VERSION (KJV): KING JAMES VERSION, public domain.

Scriptures marked AMP are taken from the AMPLIFIED BIBLE (AMP): Scripture taken from the AMPLIFIED® BIBLE, Copyright © 1954, 1958, 1962, 1964, 1965, 1987 by the Lockman Foundation Used by Permission. (www.Lockman.org)

Amari Rise Publishing
www.marilynrandolph.com
Copyright © 2019 Marilyn Randolph
All rights reserved.

Dedication

❖

I would like to dedicate this book to my family, my husband who has supported me through this journey. My children LeAndre, Giovanta, Trey, Dontay, LaRone, Brittany and daughter-in-law Ebone' who I love so very much. My Nana, and beloved Grammie Betty whom I miss dearly. To my late Auntie Minnie, Cousin Joyce, and my beloved Mother Barbara for their spiritual guidance and example of Life in Christ Jesus. My cousin Justin for his prayers, spiritual support, and encouragement to finish this book. Also My siblings Erika, Shan, Amber, Savana, Taylor, Nyrea, and Ethan. To my Father who raised me, Dennis and my Birth Father, Joseph, and to all my wonderful godchildren.

Acknowledgement

❖

I thank and praise God for all he has done in helping me to Be Still so that he can move in my life. I thank him for Lonzine Lee who is an inspiration in my life and has encouraged me and supported me through this journey of writing my book. I thank him for Deirdra Lampkins who is truly a diamond in the rough and my publishers who helped me bring this work to completion. I thank him for my Pastor Johnny Q. Jones who has been there as my spiritual Father, who has prayed for me and spoken blessings over my life, and who picked up his phone whenever I called.

Contents

❖

MARILYN M. RANDOLPH

Introduction

❖

Many years ago I thought about writing a book. I actually started one, but I never finished it. Years later, God revealed to me that it was time; it was time to testify of his goodness and glory over my life. It was time to share what he has brought me through and where he is taking me. So now that I am older and a little wiser. I am ready to write. I hope to bless someone by sharing episodes from my story. God has brought me a long way. I have written of my testimony in prayer in the hope that it will encourage you to keep going and never give up.

I want to activate healing and deliverance in your life, but most of all I want you to be saved and filled with His Holy Spirit.

I pray that this book blesses you beyond measure, and that it encourages you to break free from bondage of any kind so you can move toward your God-ordained destiny. It is my intent that this book will help someone who is building—or wants to build—a deeper and more meaningful relationship with God. I pray that you, too, find rest from all that would cause you to fret and, instead, hear His voice in Psalm

46:10 as he tells you, *"Be still, and know that I am God. I will be exalted among the nations. I will be exalted in the earth."*

Blessings,

Marilyn Randolph

Author's Note:

With the exception of my mother, Mrs. Barbara, Aunt Minnie, Gramma Christine, and Granny Betty, the names of family, friends, old boyfriends, and associates have been changed to protect their privacy.

SECTION 1

❖

WHERE DO I BEGIN WITH ALL OF THIS

❖

Truth and Challenges

"And ye shall know the truth, and the truth shall make you free." – John 8:32

A t one time or another, everyone faces challenges. Sometimes those challenges can become overwhelming, and sometimes they are too much to bear. Have you ever been there? I have.

Today, when you look at my life you will see a woman who lives with no regrets, a woman who is fulfilled with the joys of life, a woman who is free from past hurt, free from religion, and free to live life abundantly. But it was not always that way.

I am a Christian. I grew up in the church, and I want to speak my truth. Knowing the truth makes us free, and I am *now* free to expose parts of myself and my journey on these pages. I'm willing to do this so that others can have the opportunity to make the decision *to be free.*

There was a time when I was tempted to act out my feelings, to leave everything—my children, my husband, my home, my job, and all the stress—behind. I was tired of it all. I was not tired of my family. I was tired of everything I had gone through still weighing me down.

Then one day I looked into the eyes of my children and my husband, and I saw LOVE. I remembered what they meant to me. I was a mother, a wife, and a co-provider. I realized I was someone greater than the thoughts and issues that had risen inside me. That's when I knew it was time to step up to my story. I was to become the woman I was meant to be. I envisioned myself as a good wife and mother, a woman who was saved and Holy Ghost-filled, educated, and a woman of God moving by the Spirit of God.

When I was growing up my mother always told me—and still tells me today—*"You can do all things through Christ."* This may be familiar to many of you. However, if you are not familiar with those words, know this: you *can* do all things through Christ!

Writing this book has been a challenge. My children and husband have walked into the room and disturbed me many times while I was trying to write or record. But I knew I could do this, so I continued to write.

I want this book to be inspiring, encouraging, uplifting, and empowering. I want this to be what you need it to be on your journey through this life. This book is just the beginning of something new for me, and it might be the start of something new for you.

I pray that this book will take both you and me many places. But even more, I pray that it brings us all on a closer walk with God. We all face challenges and obstacles, but in Romans 8:37 the Word of God says that we are more than conquerors. Always know that you can get through whatever challenges face you. I guarantee that, with God on your side, you will have the victory.

One affirmation I tell myself every day is this: "I know I can do it because I know God is with me." It is a daily walk.

Through all that I have endured and dealt with, God has been with me. I have experienced the death of my grandmother, the sickness of my sisters, and the incarceration of my son in addition to sexual abuse, physical abuse, and church hurt. When I speak of church hurt, I'm talking about when you try to interact with people at church, but they turn away from you and talk about you behind your back. You speak to them, and they act like you don't exist. I'm talking about when people in the church judge you because you don't dress or talk like they do.

That wasn't supposed to happen—especially at church. The church is supposed to offer salvation, a refuge, and teach the word of God so we can live a Christian life. And it was like that for me at one time. But that type of church hurt can make you want to leave the church and not attend church at all. When I finally stopped looking for the acceptance of people, I found God. I just wanted to mention a few trials to say God stayed with me through it all. He guided me and, most important, He strengthened me.

The Bible actually speaks of being free. Freedom is a choice that everyone must make for themselves.

1 Corinthians 10:13 says:

> *There hath no temptation taken you but such as is common to man: but God is faithful, who will not suffer you to be tempted above that ye are able; but will with the temptation also make a way to escape, that ye may be able to bear it.*

So if God isn't overloading us and stopping us from being free, where is all of the burden coming from? I found the answer. This is the truth that I know. This is the story that I will tell on these pages, this truth that makes me FREE.

Beginnings

My beginning,
May not be like your beginning,
But beginnings are true and real.
Whether it be life.
Whether it be death
It all begins with you.
My beginning
May not be like your beginning,
But a new beginning is true.
It can be a new year, new options, new trial,
It can also **be a new you**.

Precious Memories

*"Train up a child in the way he should go: and when he is
old, he will not depart from it."*
– Proverbs 22:6

My name is Marilyn. I was born and raised in Northern California. I am the oldest of five girls and two boys. We are seven siblings, but we do not all share the same mother or father. My mother and grandmother have said ever since I was small that I was a happy, loving, and good. They said that, as an infant, I never cried a lot, and that I was very independent. That has always stuck with me.

Transplanted to California from New Orleans, my mother and her family settled in Northern California. My mother, Barbara, was sixteen and my father was fifteen when she became pregnant with me. My mother was a thin, brown-skinned, timid, and beautiful young woman. My daddy, Mr. Jay, was a well-known brother from around the way. He was known as a true ladies' man. It is my understanding that he had many women. He was young, handsome, and a major player. He was dark skinned, muscular, tall, and always dressed to a tee. I could say he was the Morris Chestnut of the 80s. I've been told that he hypnotized ladies with his handsomeness.

Aunt B, my mother's friend, introduced my parents to each other in the early 70s. While my mother fell head over heels for Jay, he treated her more like a friend than a girlfriend because she was not what he wanted. Yet not long after they met, I was on the way.

My beautiful mother, Mrs. Barbara, is one of the most loving, sweet, precious women you could ever meet. My mother is a woman who listens and comforts. She has a healing touch that is warm and nurturing. People, especially young people, love talking to her. She is everything to me; I wouldn't know what to do without her.

I really didn't know what to think of the story of her and my father's relationship when my mother told me about it. You always want the fairytale with the mother, father, and baby living happily ever after. From what I gathered, my dad was never really in love with my mother. It was more a case of him satisfying his lust for girls like most boys during that era. Come to think of it, the same was true during my era and is still true today. So Jay ran when he found out my mother was pregnant; he ducked and covered. Regardless, I was still on the way.

I am a member of Generation X. As a child growing up I had a lot of love. I never went without anything, and I remember having a lot of family around, mostly from my mother's side.

We lived in a small, three-bedroom, brown-and-beige house in the East Bay for about three years. The house had a fenced-in patio and a long driveway along the side of the house that allowed you to park and walk up the stairs into the house. I recall that if you looked out the window, you could see the driveway and front gate. When you walked into the house you would come right into the living room. The living room had a round, dark brown, furry-looking sofa. You could also see and walk right into the kitchen from the living room. There was a big backyard that was full of grass with plenty of room to play. It was a beautiful home.

Gramma Christine, my mother's mom, was a thin, high-cheek-boned woman. She said she got her caramel complexion, beautiful medium-length dark brown hair, and looks from the Apache Indian side of the family. She was sassy about herself. She was a Texan, born and raised in Fort Worth. My mother and uncle stated that was the perfect spot for them, and yes, it was also perfect for me. I loved that house. I remember it to this day.

Occasionally, I pass by it when I visit my home church, which is right down the street from my childhood home. Although it was small, the house was cozy, open, inviting, and warm. I still remember as a toddler jumping up and down on the long brown sofa in my little red dress. When people came over they all seemed right at home. There was a lot of laughter in that house, which probably contributed to the happiness I felt growing up.

One positive aspect of living in that little house was that we lived across the street from my great-great-great Aunt Minnie. Aunt Minnie was the rock and foundation of our family and the neighborhood. Her example of strength and morality encouraged the women and young ladies in our family. There were occasions when she would say to me, "Go over yonder!" What she meant was, "Girl, go over there some- where because you're bothering me." #LOL. I would then sing to her the song by Walter Hawkins, "I'm Going Up A Yonder," and she would just laugh. At times, I could be a little humorous.

Aunt Minnie looked like Mahalia Jackson to me. She was built just like Mahalia Jackson. She had big boobs and a gold tooth. She wore short wigs and glasses. She dressed sharply in long dresses. Aunt Min- nie had a high, monotonous voice. She always said, "Hey, baby," in a sweet voice with a big smile. But when you got out of line, her voice would get raspy and loud. When we would act up or cut up, as they say, she would whoop our behinds.

Aunt Minnie was the matriarch of our family, and she did not play. This was especially true when it came to God and family. She was always watching us, and she was always there for us spiritually to provide nurturing, direction, and discipline when needed. She was the very core of my mother's side of the family.

Aunt Minnie was amazing. Not only did she raise her own children, but she also helped raise my grandmother, my momma, and me. She was always active in and around our lives. Aunt Minnie was truly a woman who took care to teach that which is good. And her teaching has played a significant role in my life.

Aunt Minnie would not let us get out of line. She was one of the eldest members of the Little Flock Church of God in Christ Church (COGIC). She was a holy, upright, virtuous woman. She was the mother of the church and a leader. She was a prayer warrior and was faithful to the church in many ways.

One thing I vividly remember about Aunt Minnie was that she was a true and faithful fan of the World Wrestling Federation (WWF, now the WWE). She and I would watch it on Sundays after church. I didn't care for it much, but I enjoyed spending time with her watching it because she would yell at the wrestlers on the TV as if they could hear her. That was so funny. I saw all of this as a child, and I still remember it so very well.

As a child I attended church with Aunt Minnie, my mother, and my cousin Joyce. Aunt Minnie stayed in church, so it was inevitable that I would be there too. Little Flock was right down the street. When I was a child, Little Flock was always packed. There were people in the pews, in the pulpit, everywhere. It felt like the church was full of the Holy Spirit, and it was flowing through the atmosphere. Little Flock was a holy and respectable place of worship. There were always people shouting, dancing, and praising God. My church was considered a holiness church. It was a hand-clapping, foot-stomping, tongues-talking, Pentecostal COGIC. When you walked through the doors of Little Flock, you felt the presence of God.

I remember many times when Joyce, who had a hand in raising me along with the rest of my family, and I walked to church. We would talk about church and family. Joyce was a constant in my life for many years, even when I moved to the South Bay.

That little house on that little block was where it all began for me when talking about both church and family. The church was within walking distance. It was a little white-and-burgundy, single-story building with a sign on the front.

Once you walked up the two long steps, there were two wooden red doors. Once inside the doors, you'd be in the foyer. The foyer led you directly into the church where there were red pews on both sides. At the front of the church there were chairs on the left where the mothers and missionaries of the church sat. The choir sat on the other side. If you walked straight down the aisle you saw the offering table. The pulpit sat behind the offering table. On the side of the pulpit were the organ and piano, both of which my godmother, the church musician, played. There was a long mirror where she would sit. She could see the choir director and receive direction on what to play next. There were fans that turned round and round on the ceiling. As a little girl I would lean back in the pew and look at them. I would fall asleep while watching them sometimes. I also recall the stained glass windows that had to be cranked open.

My Sunday school was in the church dining room. The Primary A Class ranged from ages five to eleven. That was Mother Johnson's Class. She was a strict, serious Sunday school teacher who had a firm voice. I made sure I paid close attention in Sunday school because she did not play when it came to teaching us about the Bible. She asked plenty of questions and always had a ruler in her hand. That ruler was called "The Rod of Correction." She would pop your hand with it when you got out of line or weren't paying attention in Sunday school. When she gave you one or two pops with the ruler, the sting made you act right really quickly. I made sure I did learn something in those Sunday school classes. But there were times when I got the ruler, and I wasn't the only one.

My Grandmothers

" . . . and that older women likewise be reverent in behavior . . . teachers of that which is good . . ." – Titus 2:3

When I was born, my father, Jay, did not even bother to come and see me. He didn't even tell his mother that he had a baby girl. I don't know all the details, but I know that my fraternal grandmothers didn't know about me. But somehow his mother, my Grammie Betty, and his grandmother, my Nana, found out about me through a mutual friend.

Well, as soon as they found out there was a baby girl, Grammie Betty and Nana came from the South Bay to the East Bay to meet me. The mutual friend who told Grammie Betty and Nana about me also told my mother to be expecting a visit from them. That is how my mother told me the story. Out of nowhere, a car suddenly pulled up into the driveway, and Grammie Betty jumped out the car and came running to the door. She couldn't wait to see me. She even left poor Nana behind running for the door. My mother said that when they knocked on the door she politely asked, "Who is it?" My Grammie Betty yelled, "It's Betty Howard, Jay's mother!" When my mother opened the door, Grammie Betty excitedly said, "I heard my son had a baby, and I want to see her!"

I was about six months old. I was on the sofa playing with toys as babies do. Grammie Betty grabbed me from the sofa and fell in love. Having their first granddaughter was a special moment for both Grammie Betty and Nana. I was told they were excited and overjoyed to see me. They talked about what a beautiful baby I was. My mother said it was as if my grandmothers were thinking "Isn't She Lovely" (by Stevie Wonder). They were in love with me from first sight. It would be a moment that my mother would never forget. After that day Grammie Betty met me, she never left my life. She was determined to make sure that my mother, Gramma Christine, and I would be taken care of.

Interestingly, my father and mother hooked up again. My mother went down to visit my father and his parents. Then when my grandparents went away, my mother and my father had sex. This was a shock to the family because Grammie Betty trusted both of them. She thought it would be okay to leave them alone. She was disappointed by it all. However, regardless of how she felt about it, it did happen. Less than two years after I was born, my baby sister Ms. E. appeared in the world. My sister came, and my mother was then a single mother with two children.

Grammie Betty, a take-charge woman, was a beautiful, dark-skinned queen who only stood about five feet tall. She was well dressed and had lovely skin and a beautiful smile. She radiated power. She had a medium-sized afro. She was loving and supportive. She was always classy and in control. Grammie Betty helped my mom and Gramma Christine move closer to her family. We became the first tenants to move into a new apartment complex that she liked. She loved the complex's name—The Pensacola Apartments. That name was significant to my grandparents because their hometown was Pensacola, Florida.

A Village Community

When we first moved into the Pensacola Apartments, it was a beautiful community of Black folks. It housed the Colas Child Development Center, a daycare center. That was highly innovative for 1976.

The director/owner of the child development center was a good friend of both my grandmothers. Nana worked in the center's kitchen, cooking up meals for the children, and my Grammie Betty worked for the Black Council, helping young black youths get their GEDs and move on to a better future.

There was a true village environment during that time. In those days many people got the help they needed from each other to keep advancing. That community of Blacks did more for one another in a true spirit of unity, brotherhood, and love than people do today. I admit to being a bit nostalgic as this is not something as apparent in our twenty-first-century communities.

Grammie Betty had her hands in so many things that I can't remember them all. She was deeply involved in her community and kept me involved. As a child I was on the drill team at the Mayfair Community Center and in African dancing at one of the elementary schools on the east side.

The drill team was a team of little girls that would perform dance routines. You would normally see them perform at colleges and high school events. For me, it was a community thang. We weren't competitive. We were just active and involved. I was around six years old at this time. I remember my white boots with the tassels, my gray skirt, and white shirt. Wooow! I was cute, and my hair was always on point, whether it was braided or in curls.

When I performed I would wear my hair out. My mother, or one of her friends, would put grease or Johnson & Johnson's baby lotion on my hair. My hair would just curl up, and I was ready to go. I also remember being involved in an African dance group with a man named Mr. Roosevelt. He was a professional and didn't play when it came to African dancing. I was a little older then, around eleven. Man, oh man, Mr. Roosevelt worked you down to the bone. But when we showed up, we always showed out. We danced at several schools in the local area and at festivals. Those days will always be some of the best memories of my childhood.

Every year during the 1980s we would have parades in downtown in celebration of Juneteenth, the commemoration of the end of slavery in the United States. It was also the day that I could be seen walking down Santa Clara Street in the celebration parade, performing with my drill teammates. I remember marching and seeing all of the people shouting and praising. It was exciting, and it made you feel proud to be BLACK! Those were special years, and I cherish those great and wonderful days of my childhood. I don't recall if the drill team was a part of the African American Center or a part of the Parks and Recreation program. Regardless, Grammie Betty made sure I was involved. She also put me in taekwondo, cheerleading, talent shows, and whatever else there was to keep me busy. I was always doing something.

My momma also got me involved in a lot of activities, but they were more spiritual. Even after we moved, I remained active in the church. Joyce would come down to pick us up and take us to Little Flock.

I remember singing a song that my sister and I made up in the bathroom called "I Want to Walk with Jesus." We sang it during one of our Youth Day events at our church. We were so nervous, but we did it for the glory and honor of God. I remember the church and getting high in the spirit while singing our song. Those were the good old days, and I will never forget those times. I loved singing to the Lord. I was never a professional, but I sang to God whether it was at church or in my bathroom. I must admit that I love to sing. Like I said before, I'm not a professional or even all that great, but I know the Lord loves it.

At church I sang in the Sunshine Band, read minutes, and played the drums. I attended Young People Willing Workers (YPWW) and Sunday school. I was always in some kind of children's play, and both E and I stayed busy in the church.

When I was about twelve we started attending a new church for a short time. It was closer to our home in the South Bay and had many young people in attendance. The pastor (God rest his soul) had a lot of children. They were as involved as I was and fun to be around. I developed a friendship with most of them.

I liked attending that church. I sang in the youth choir, played the drums, and tried but never really mastered the piano. Later, I was appointed to teach Sunday school for my age group along with one of the pastor's sons. It was a challenge in itself, but I did it. I continued until my world got turned around.

My Mother, MyWorld

"Who can find a virtuous woman? For her price is far above rubies." – Proverbs 31:10

M y mother is a baby boomer who was born in the late 50s along with her younger brother in New Orleans, Louisiana. Their father was New Orleans Creole, meaning that he was French and Black. In those days of the 50s my mother was called a dark-skinned Creole, and my uncle was a light-skinned Creole. People made a difference between those with light-skin and those with dark-skin. Light-skinned blacks were made to feel superior to dark-skinned blacks. But those with dark-skin where looked down on and treated as if they were beneath the others.

Momma told me that even the birth certificates identified light- and dark-skinned Creoles with a big C for light-skinned Creoles and little c representing dark-skinned Creoles. This was the skin color game.

The conflict of light skin vs. dark skin was a big issue in the Southern black community. It's sad to think about blacks being racist against each other because of skin color. However, this didn't stop my mother. Even though she was dark skinned, she was happy and carefree. She had no worries about being treated differently because of her skin. She was well taken care of by her parents, Joseph and Christine Jackson.

Growing up, my mother dressed up, especially during Mardi Gras. She told me the story of the blue can-can dress she wore during the Mardi Gras parade. She pranced down the streets with her parents in the parade, picking up coins and beads. She said she loved Mardi Gras, and it was one of her most memorable experiences from growing up in New Orleans.

Mr. Joseph Jackson, my mother's father, used to dance on street corners downtown for a living and would bring home good money. Those were special years that my mother could recall while growing up. My mother said that her mother and father took such good care of her, and she never saw anything out of the ordinary. However, she felt there were things that were wrong. One of the issues that was prevalent was her mother's alcoholism. My mother also found out through the family that her father had been abusive toward her mother. My mother never saw the abuse, but family members would speak about it. My mother was very young at the time. The physical abuse that my grandmother, Gramma Christine, suffered led her to make some decisions that would change my mother's and uncle's lives forever.

I was told that one day my grandmother called her brother, my great Uncle Sunny and his wife Ester, for help. She said she wanted to leave New Orleans. My Great Uncle Sunny already knew about the abuse my grandmother was dealing with, so he drove from California to New Orleans. He and Aunt Ester picked up my grandmother and her children and took them away. They all left New Orleans for California and never looked back. My mother was seven when they left. She really didn't know what to expect when moving to a new place, but she was ready. They moved to Northern California and began their new life.

Once in California, My mother and her family moved in with Uncle Sunny. Unfortunately, nothing had changed with my Gramma Christine's alcoholism. At one point it got so bad they had to put her in a rehab program at Agnews Developmental Center. Agnews was a center for mentally challenged individuals. It offered programs that would help my Gramma Christine with her alcohol problem.

While my grandmother was in Agnews my mother and uncle continued to stay with Uncle Sunny. They would visit their mother at the Agnews Developmental Center. My mother could remember visiting on holidays. It took a while for Gramma Christine to recover, but she stayed sober for some time after she left Agnews.

When Gramma Christine got out of the program, she and her children moved in with one of my Gramma Christine's relatives. This relative owned a tow yard and had a little tin house in the back. That is where my mother, uncle, and Gramma Christine lived for a year until she found out about a housing program and moved into their own home. It was the little brown house where I lived as a baby.

After living in that house for some years, when my mother got older, my grandma started to drink again. When she drank she would go to her friends' houses and get sloppy drunk. She would be laid out at different locations. Her favorite things to drink were Coors and Thunderbird. If her friends made her mad, she would cuss them out. Momma told me she thought Gramma Christine started drinking when she lived in New Orleans, but she never knew why. My mother said she had a really good childhood despite the obstacles they had to face. They stuck together through it all.

Years later, after moving to the South Bay, my mother got word that her father was in prison for stealing. My mother had no connection with him until sometime in the late 80s. One day, out of nowhere, he called and asked my mother to buy him a watch. Now, of course, she felt stunned because she barely even knew this man, and he was asking her for some material item. He wasn't calling to see her. He wasn't calling wanting to get to know her. He didn't want to build a relationship with his daughter with whom he had no interaction since she was seven years old. Well, after that conversation, my mother was done with him. From that day forward, she lost contact with him.

Then, in August 2005 after Hurricane Katrina had hit New Orleans, with the assistance of the Red Cross I got a hold of him. But in actuality, we are not even sure it was him. The Red Cross connected us with a severely ill man in a senior home in Baton Rouge. Because he was too ill to speak, we never knew if it was him or not. However, that would be the last time we ever heard about my mother's father.

Meanwhile, still looking back at my mother's childhood, when she speaks of her dad, it is a man named Mr. White. The story I was told about Mr. White was that he was a sophisticated man who was well dressed and groomed. He was of a medium build, light-skinned, and spent a lot of money on their family. This is the man who helped raise my mother and uncle. He was good to my Gramma Christine and her children too. He was a military man and a great provider for the family. My mother was especially fond of him, but she said there was something mentally wrong with the man. She said he would do crazy things every six months on the dot. For instance, Mr. White wanted to take Gramma Christine and the kids to a San Francisco Giants baseball game. As they drove on the freeway to the game, he suddenly stopped the car in the middle of the freeway. He got out of the car and stopped all the cars behind them. When asked what he was doing, he said he was a police officer directing traffic. He wouldn't get back into the car. My mother said she and her brother were so embarrassed that they slid down in the back seat and hid so people passing couldn't see them. It was later found out that he was suffering from Post Trumatic Stress Disorder from being in the military. Other than his rare outbursts, they had a pretty good life with Mr. White. However, he and Gramma Christine parted ways after a few years. My mother grew up and came into her own. When she was fifteen, she met Mr. Jay, and I made my grand entrance soon after that meeting.

Today, my mother and I have a close relationship. We always have and always will. She married Dennis, who became my dad. My dad was funny. There were times he would get out the car while we were going somewhere and do crazy things like walk funny or make a funny face, and we would just laugh. Dad spent a lot of time with us. We went fishing, to basketball games, to whatever. He made time for us.

My sister and I had a good relationship with our dad. Because of him, I learned what a true father—and man—was. He was and is the best father a young lady could ever want. He raised my sister and me. He and my mother then added a baby brother to our family. Dennis, my dad, coined the saying, "The only steps in our house were the ones at the front door." This meant that we were all family, and the word "step" was not allowed. That was profound and made me feel whole now that I had a father who loved and wanted me.

Interestingly, my mother married a military man, and so did I. Might I add that my uncle was in the military. My Grammie Betty married a military man, and so did my Nana. I just felt the need to say this because military men have always been a part of our family. These people, my family, have been inspirational, strong, prayerful, and influential. I am a product of all of them.

Those women loved me and planted seeds in me by showing me and teaching me how to be a caretaker, a parent and missionary. I was able to grow and become a woman because I grew up seeing what true women were like. Those concepts helped me raise my family and be all I could be in the lives of my children, my community, and my church.

Those seeds would help me, especially during the things I went through during my childhood and young adult years. I shudder to think what would have become of me if I hadn't gotten those seeds early in life.

SECTION 2

❖

THE GOOD, THE BAD & THE UGLY

CHAP TER FIVE

❖

Innocence Shattered

My birth father was never around much when I was a young girl, so I never really got to know him. He was always in and out of jail. But I really didn't think it mattered because I had someone who was always around. Mr. Dennis stepped in as my father and became the dad who raised me. He was a great dad. He was a military man who was stationed at Fort Ord, California, a military base in Seaside/Monterey, California. My mother met him while clubbing.

From the onset Mr. Dennis stepped in and became the man my mother needed and wanted. He also became the father to my little sister, Ms. E, and me that we needed. It was not long afterward that my little brother, Mr. Maurice, appeared.

Mr. Dennis took us fishing and on picnics, among other activities. Every Independence Day we would go to Moffett Field to see the jets and watch the fireworks. My dad was great.

One of my friends from a school I attended recognized Mr. Dennis on the bus one day. They said, "Hey, you're Marilyn's stepdad." He told them the only steps in our house were the ones at the front door. (Smile) He was a good and protective father.

#Stepsarenotfamily

Steps are what you take to move up or down, not to define your relationship within your family. While my dad was in the military he would often come home during leave. One time while he was gone my mother moved out of the apartments where we lived because she wanted to get away from my grandmother. They were having issues regarding my grandmother's alcoholism and her aggression toward my dad.

My mother, sister, and I moved in with one of my mother's friends, Ms. CeeCee, when I was about seven years old. Ms. CeeCee was a dark-skinned lady with braids that went down her back. When she didn't have braids she would wear her hair short. Ms. CeeCee was a medium-built woman who was around 5'6" tall with a kind of pointy nose. She had two daughters who were around the same age as my sister and me. When we moved in with them it seemed like everything would work out okay. Everything started out fine. My sister and I got along great with the girls, and my mother got along great with Ms.

CeeCee. However, over time things ended up not working out so well.

Ms. CeeCee was stingy with food. If my mother didn't have food for us, Ms. CeeCee wouldn't let us have anything. She literally would have let us starve. I recall one incident when we were about to eat cereal, but we had no milk. Ms. CeeCee would not let us have any of her milk. As a result, we had to eat our cereal with water. My mother probably could have called one of my grandmothers for help, but instead she said, "We are going to make it. It's fine. Just eat the cereal with water." It was rough on my mother, but she did what she had to do for us. She tried to make the best choices for us as a family.

Ms. CeeCee also had a boyfriend. We'll call him Chuck. He also lived in the house, and it was awful because he kept trying to push himself onto my mother. He even came into my mother's room naked one night, trying to persuade her to have sex with him. When he came into her room my mother yelled, "Get out of here and leave me alone!" She vowed to tell Ms. CeeCee. After that night, he no longer tried anything with my mother. However, my mother didn't feel comfortable, so she swallowed her pride and moved back in with Gramma Christine.

When my dad found out about the things Mr. Chuck had done, he was very upset. Dad did not like the fact that Chuck was pushing himself on his woman. He made his feelings known to Mr. Chuck. I don't know the details of what happened because I was an adult when I heard the story, but let's just say that after that Mr. Chuck didn't bother my mother anymore.

I don't recall my exact age at the time, but I believe I was around eight when the drama played out with my mom, dad, and Mr. Chuck. Not knowing the story of Mr. Chuck and my mother, I viewed him as "a friend of the family." I thought I could trust him, and I wasn't told anything otherwise.

One day this same "friend of the family" came to the apartments where we lived. I was outside playing with my friends on the other side of the complex when Mr. Chuck asked me to come with him. He asked me to get into his car. Not thinking anything of it, I obeyed; after all, it was Mr. Chuck, and I considered him a friend. It was a hot summer day, so I got into his car thinking he had something good for me. I had no idea what he was about to do to me. I remember now that, after I got into his car, he had an especially weird look. His eyes seemed almost evil. His voice was twisted, and he was talking strangely. I began to feel uncomfortable and scared. I stared at him in shock. I didn't know what was going to happen, but I knew something felt off.

Mr. Chuck put his hands between my legs and started to touch my private parts. I don't remember what he said because I went blank. It felt weird, and I got real uncomfortable. I started to cry loudly. Suddenly, with a loud and aggressive voice he yelled, "Get out of my car!" I jumped out as fast as I could, and then he drove away.

After I had gotten out of the car, I stood there shaking and in shock. The world seemed to continue to move around me, but I stood there in a trance. At that moment I felt shame, like I had done something wrong. Then I suddenly felt lost and confused. I felt like something had left me. Even more shock kicked in, and I didn't understand what had just happened to me, but I knew it didn't feel right.

Suddenly, reality hit me like a ton of bricks. All of the energy that had once left my body and had forbade me to move came rushing back all at once. I started screaming. I screamed so loud, over and over. Other kids and a lady came running to see what had happened. The lady didn't know what had happened, but she could tell something was seriously wrong, so she told me to go home fast. I ran home as fast as my eight-year-old legs could carry me. As soon as I saw my mom, I ran into her arms crying and told her what had happened with Mr. Chuck. From that point on everything became a blur. However, I did find out later that my Uncle Emmett and my Dad had gone looking for Mr. Chuck all over the city, but he had disappeared.

I also remember a police officer coming to my home and recording my account of what Mr. Chuck did to me that day. I believe he went to jail, but I'm not sure because I never saw him again. I always believed the demon that scared me that day would also hurt and torment him for the rest of his life.

Tears come to my eyes when I thought of my molestation. But as I purged and wrote about the depth of this story in these pages, I was able to free myself from my past completely. I have been healed from the inside out. I realized that eight-year-old Marilyn's story needed to be told, and only adult Marilyn could do that. I am healed, and I am delivered. I don't have to dwell on it, but I do want to testify about it. We are healed through our testimony, and I want you to be healed.

I have compassion for young children who have gone through similar situations. It's so sad that any child should ever have to experience something like that. I pray that those children all will be healed and delivered from such perversion. I understand and pray this book helps in the healing process.

I didn't know it at that time, but God was ordering my steps, even as a little girl. From that day forward I kept moving; I didn't let what that man did affect my footsteps.

#Thedevildidnothavehisvictory

I was going to be a witness, a testimony to someone. My parents were put on this earth to raise me in a way that would help me help others. As I continued to grow, the knowledge of helping others became more and more obvious.

When I First Heard God Speak To Me

As a child in middle school I remember a girl who I thought was my friend. But for some odd reason she started to bully me out of nowhere, or so I thought. I was always outgoing and friendly, but there were also times when I defended my friends.

I was around twelve when the Lord filled me with the Holy Ghost. I was trying to live right in His sight. For no reason whatsoever, that girl told me she was going to whoop me the last day of school. She said it was just because she wanted to. She was a big girl too. It was going to be a David and Goliath fight. I went home and told my mother about the problem. I had hoped she would defend me and talk with someone at the school about it, but she did the opposite: she told me to go into my room and pray.

I looked at her and began to cry, saying, *"Pray?"*

She calmly said, "Go and talk to God. He will deliver you."

I did just that. I went to my room and fell on my knees in prayer.

I cried and prayed, prayed and cried, and then I heard a whispering voice in my ear that said, "Do you trust Me?"

I turned to the scripture, Psalms 3:1-8, and it said:

"Lord, how are they increased that trouble me: many are they that rise up against me. 2. Many there be which say of my soul, there is no help for him in God. Selah. 3. But thou, O Lord, art a shield for me; my glory, and the lifter up of mine head. 4. I cried unto the Lord with my voice, and he heard me out of his holy hill. Selah. 5. I laid me down and slept; I awaked; for the Lord sustained me. 6. I will not be afraid of then thousands of people that have set themselves against me round about. 7. Arise, O Lord; save me, O my God: for thou hast smitten all mine enemies upon the cheek bone; thou hast broken the teeth of the ungodly. 8. Salvation belongeth unto the Lord: thy blessing us upon the people. Selah."

Trusting in God, I knew no harm would come to me.

I went to school on the last day. I was on the baseball field with my friends, giving them hugs and love, when a crowd of people started to come my way. I looked up to see all of these people following the girl who had threatened me. She approached to see me and my friends crying and hugging. She walked directly up to me. As I faced her, she asked, "What are you crying for?"

I told her, "Because I'm going to miss my friends." I paused and then said, "And I'm going to miss you too." Suddenly, I opened my arms wide like Jesus saying, "Come unto me," turned my head sideways, and reached out to give her a hug. I didn't know what she would do. I just stood there. She paused, looking at me strangely. She then smiled, opened her arms and, to my surprise, she hugged me too. Neither of us realized God knew what she needed, and He used me to give it to her. Love conquers all.

#smile

When you have the love of Christ within you, it resonates. I gave her the love of God. When she received it, she also began to weep and apologized. We became true friends, even through our freshman year of high school.

That was my first encounter with God. It showed me that prayer works when you talk to Him from your heart. He will hear you and deliver you.

#WhenGodspeaksjustlisten

Discussion Questions

(Take time to think about these.)

When you look back on this story, what did you get from it?

How did it inspire you?

How can it help you?

❖

Bruised, Yes; Broken, No!

In the early 80s I had spent some time going back and forth between my mom and Grammie Betty's houses. I had some relatives who lived directly across from Grammie Betty. It was nice because I had cousins right there across the street.

It was my Nana's niece Patty and four of her six children (Danita, Stacy, Stan, and Rob). Two of my cousins reminded me of the children from the 70s TV show *Good Times*. My cousin Danita, who always dressed to impress, had a style like no one else. She dressed like the ladies from Prince's group the Revolution, and her hair was always on fleek (what the young people say today). Danita was like Thelma: she had style, class, and beauty.

My cousin Stan reminded me of JJ. He could be funny, and he was tall and lanky. He played basketball and was really good at it. He wore Converse high tops with red-striped, knee-high socks.

Stacy really didn't remind me of anyone. She was just kind and sweet. She was also tall, but she was not lanky like Stan. She was tall and pretty like a model. She had short hair and was not as outgoing as Danita. She loved laughing and was quiet until you upset her.

Rob was also tall and thin. He was dark-skinned and had a funny look. He didn't have the good looks like the rest of his family. He looked and acted odd. He always had a goofy look about him. He had big eyes and a smirk at times. He was mean and nasty, and I didn't like to be around him at all.

I loved my cousin Stacy. She always spent time with me and treated me really well. She was like a big sister. In fact, all of them were nice to me—except for Rob. I was always uneasy around him. I was always uncomfortable and restless. He was always mean to me. He would push me out the way when passing by. Most of the time he used a mean tone when he spoke to me. My cousin Stacy would often tell him to leave me alone, but he didn't listen. If I went into their room to say hi to his brother Stan, Rob would yell at me to get out. I tried my best to stay out of his way.

I was maybe eleven when Rob sexually abused me. It was one of the times when I went across the street to visit Stacey. On that particular day Rob was unusually nice to me, which was odd. I thought he had changed when he politely invited me to come into the house. I had come, as usual, to see Stacey, but he didn't tell me Stacy wasn't home.

I went into the house and asked, "Where is Stacy?" He said, "She was in her room." He had an ugly smirk.

I went toward her room, and he followed me. That was weird and completely unusual. I thought, "This is strange," but I kept walking toward her room.

Once I walked inside her room and didn't see Stacy. I turned and asked Rob, "Where is she?" That's when he pushed me down. I fell on her bed, and he hit me. Stunned, I had no idea what and why he was doing that. I said, "What are you doing?" I thought my voice would cause him to see me. He kept saying something, but I was so shocked by his hitting me that I couldn't understand what he was saying. It was like being under water.

I was panicking. Frightened and scared, I lay there too afraid to move; I did not move or scream. I was terrified. Every second felt like an eternity. My heart was beating so fast and hard. As he held me down, he put his hand over my mouth and climbed on top of me. I looked right into his eyes, hoping that he would see me—his cousin. He never looked into my eyes. He continued as he inappropriately started to touch my private area and pulled his penis out. My eyes filled with tears. He gyrated over me and began moving his penis up and down my private area. Hot tears ran down the sides of my face as I lay there hurt and in pain.

I cried as I remembered what had happened with Mr. Chuck. I was feeling helpless, wondering why this was happening to me again. What had I done to deserve this abuse? This was my cousin, my blood.

"THIS IS NOT SUPPOSED TO HAPPEN!" I screamed in my mind.

I was stuck in time. Frozen in my mind. I came back as I felt hot liquid land all over me. Still never saying a word I thought, "What the heck is that?" Then Rob got up, pulled his pants up, and walked out of the room like nothing had happened. I stayed motionless on the bed for a moment, still frazzled. Suddenly realizing I was free, I sat up. I looked at the runny liquid all over me, grabbed my cousin's blanket, and wiped the liquid off. I pulled my pants up as fast as I could and ran out of there. I could think of nothing except getting away.

I ran straight back to Grammie Betty's house and into the bathroom to clean myself off. I was still in shock and crying as I cleaned myself and changed my clothes. I cried more and more, now questioning if it was my fault.

I became depressed around this age. I tried to figure out why these males were hurting me in this way. I could not understand why they were doing this to me. I didn't know about sex or anything at the point of those violations of my privacy. I just knew it wasn't right. I was an innocent child. I was a funny, loving, caring, and outgoing child. The past hurt was gone, but this new violation brought back all the memories of Mr. Chuck. And this time, the violator was my fifteen-year-old relative.

I kept asking myself, "Why? Why? Why was this happening?"

I remember thinking that I couldn't trust any male ever again. My innocence had been stolen—not once, but twice. And that was two times too many.

I don't recall the day when I told my Grammie about what had happened. However, I remember feeling like she didn't believe me. She didn't respond, nor did she react like my mother had when everything happened with Mr. Chuck. In fact, I didn't see anything happening. No one talked to me about it, nor did I hear anything more about it. I was numb for a while. I felt like no one cared. The world kept moving around me, but I was standing still in my own personal trauma.

I never knew what Grammie did, but I didn't see Rob anymore. He was just suddenly gone one day. Then shortly afterward, his entire family ended up moving. I wouldn't see Rob again until his mother's death. By that time, we were both adults. He spoke, and I spoke back.

We never exchanged any more words. There was nothing else to say.

Even though he never apologized or even acknowledged what he had done, it happened. I remember. Yet I have forgiven him, and I no longer allow myself to be victimized by that event.

Praise God!

"Therefore, if any man be in Christ, he is a new creature: old things are passed away; behold all things are become new." – 2 Corinthians 5:17

Sitting here and going back in time really helps me realize how far God has brought me. As a child I was bruised, *but I was not broken.* I continue to grow in this spiritual walk, and I thank Him through this testimony for bringing me out of the past. I don't live in my past anymore. THANK YOU, JESUS!

#thepastisjustthat

The enemy will continually try to discourage you and try to make you live in your past of hurt and pain. But I'm here to tell you that when you leave the past in the past, it will no longer take root in your life, and you will LIVE.

"If the Son therefore shall make you free, ye shall be free indeed."
– John 8:36

#GlorybetoGod

"The thief cometh not, but for to steal, and to kill, and to destroy: I am come that they might have it more abundantly." – John 10:10

CHAPTER SEVEN

❖

Church Girl & Middle School

s a young girl I was athletic, sporty, talkative, outgoing, and friendly. I gravitated to people who were different from me. Actually, I was a bit protective of them. Truthfully, although I was quite active, I still felt a little different. However, there were times I would try to be mean to people. There were always those who tried to act tough. Then there were those who thought they were better than others. During those times I was feeling hurt and pain from things I was going through. I felt like I had to defend others. I needed to defend them for all the times that no one had defended me.

A lot of my emotional outbursts stemmed from being violated as a young girl. But the outbursts also came from a lack of confidence. I was bothered by people talking about the gap in my teeth or being too dark skinned. It was hard for me, and I tried to fit in but I *felt like* I was always out of the loop with the "in" crowd.

I was always in church. Now I loved the Lord and loved going to church, but children at my school weren't into church life. They were into dressing "fly and fresh," being popular, relationships, smoking weed, and break dancing.

During that time my grandmother kept me dressed in all the latest fashions. I had my Adidas shoes and sweat suits. I wore my Gazelles, bamboo earrings, and Kangol hats. I even had colored contact lenses. Grammie Betty hooked me up.

I learned how to break dance, and then I became a little popular, which made me feel like I was cool. But still I was also called a church girl because I loved to talk about the Lord. I tried really hard to fit in, but it just didn't work. I went to see all the music greats: New Edition, Run DMC, LL Cool J, Whodini, and Slick Rick. I used to brag about it. I had the shirts with their names on them and rode in limos to their concerts. I'm telling you, Grammie Betty did it up for my sister and I. But even with all of that, I was never able to fit in.

Middle school was rough. It was a constant roller coaster ride. One minute I tried hard and was popular. The next minute I was **a nobody**. I really couldn't keep up. I even tried to have a boyfriend, but having a boyfriend didn't make me popular nor did it fix my real problems.

One big challenge was being a born-again Christian at thirteen. I didn't really understand what I could and couldn't do. It all seemed fun and innocent. I was listening to what everyone from the church was saying. They all had an opinion about what was and wasn't righteous. I never read the Word (the Holy Bible) for myself. I heard it from others and their views of it.

According to the elders of my church I was a "backslider" from the faith. They said things like if I wore pants, lipstick, and short-sleeved shirts, I wasn't saved. I couldn't even walk into a liquor store just to buy gum. I tried to fit in at my church in other ways. I became more active in church activities. I read the minutes in Sunday school, played the drums, tried to play the piano. I sang with the Sunshine Band in the Youth Choir. I was also part of the usher's board and performed in children's plays during the holidays. I was involved in a lot of things. It was encouraging at times to be active in the church because it helped me build a foundation that I would need later in my life.

I learned that it wasn't about what I wore nor about what I did. It was about who I was on the inside. It isn't easy to say that the people at church were totally wrong when they challenged the younger people on our attire, but it was put out there the wrong way. Because I was so young and did not fully understand God's love, I was manipulated into believing that God no longer wanted me as part of His Kingdom because of my attire, which was not true. God knows us inside out. He even knows the number of hairs on our head. That means he knows everything, including our hearts:

"But even the very hairs of your head are all numbered. Fear not, therefore:

ye are of more value than many sparrows." – Luke 12:7

I can say there were some traditions that my church was big on. The only time you were able to "come as you are" was when you were a visitor trying to find a church home. After you became a member of the church, you were required to dress and become active in the church. That was the COGIC way of life.

Today, I understand what those in the church were trying to do. They were trying to separate the COGIC folks from the worldly folks.

#youfitinwithhim

#Be*ing

I went through a lot of emotional issues while I was trying to fit in. That was especially true because I was different from the rest. I was taught that when you're in Christ, you will take shape and fit yourself into His way, not the way of the world. When you were saved as a young person in the church, everyone looks up to you. You were supposed to be changed and become a new person. But it also meant if you made a mistake it would be known throughout the whole church and people outside the church. You were either saved or not. Back then I struggled in my walk with Christ. Today, there is no struggle because I know who I am in Christ.

Our relationship with God is an individual affair. You have to love the Lord to really understand His Holiness. It's more than a fashion show with the hats, names, titles, and positions. Loving the Lord is about true holy living.

"...but as He who called you is holy, you also be holy in all your conduct, [16] because it is written, "Be holy, for I am holy." – 1 Peter 1:15-16

This is a valuable lesson that we must learn. Don't worry about how you look when you walk in the door; just walk in the door. He will clean you up if you need cleaning. He will make you whole. It's not about anything other than Him.

Just Walk Through The Door.

It says in Isaiah 1:18:

"Come now, and let us reason together, saith the Lord; though your sins be as scarlet, they shall be as white as snow; though they be red like crimson, they shall be as wool."

Romans 10:13 tells us, *"For whosoever shall call upon the name of the Lord shall be saved."*

As an adult, I do realize how things and people change, but I know something else: as we are told in Malachi 3:6, God never changes.

I have one last observation of my middle school years. I used to break dance, pop lock, and groove really well. And you know what? I enjoyed it. It was fun. I enjoyed battling and showing off my skills. I wasn't doing sexy dances or anything like that. I was dancing as an art. It wasn't my heart's intention to sin against God. I really loved the Lord, and I didn't want to disrespect Him in any way. So I didn't understand why people were making me feel like He didn't love me anymore because of it. At the time I questioned what was wrong with break dancing. That's what I really wanted to know. I really didn't understand, and there was no one to help me understand.

I was starting to feel like there was no fun in being saved. I felt like there was nothing to encourage me at that time in my life. There was nothing telling me to keep pushing. That was a challenge I had to face as a young girl. It was also a decision that I had to make for myself. Why? Because I had to learn how to walk, and that walk was sometimes going to be a challenge.

"Whether therefore ye eat, or drink, or whatsoever ye do, do all to the Glory of God." – 1 Corinthians 10:31

There were times when I felt like I was in a box or bubble. I started feeling restless. Being young, I would just say what came to mind. I should have known better. Always be careful what you say because you never know how someone is going to react. It was clear that I needed something. I needed Jesus. The enemy had taken over and started to deceive me. Many events started to happen to me. Those events would turn out to be traumas that would haunt me forever.

#theyonlywantedtohelp

#Ihadtoseeformyself

After those events I started to see things, things that I never understood, things that my parents and the church tried to keep me from. Those things would send my life out of control. Those things would cause me to experience even more trauma than I already had.

❖

High School and Low Living

High school introduced me to a different kind of pressure. It opened the door to things like drugs, sex, cutting classes, and house parties. At times I was terribly confused. During that time my peers and I really cared about popularity and who had the best outfits or gear. I recall my homegirls and I (that's what we would call each other back then) would talk about the latest fashion, such as bamboo earrings and Jordache jeans, how banging our Jheri curls had to be, and who all was on point with their attire. We were trying to be what LL Cool J called "around the way" girls. We would be like, "Girl, did you see who was on *Video Soul* last night?" It would be Klymaxx, Salt and Pepa, MC Lyte, En Vogue, Queen Latifah, Yo-Yo, and a host of other artists that we liked then, the late 80s to the early 90s. Those were my high school years.

We wore Africa medallions and Mercedes-Benz and BMW emblems on chains around our necks. We also wore polka dots and lime or bright orange clothing. Then people started to wear gang colors. They wore red and blue rags and outfits. They claimed neighborhoods with those colors.

Our music went from black awareness like De La Soul, Queen Latifah, KRS-One, and Public Enemy to gangster music like NWA, Geto Boys, Ice-T, and Too $hort. Things were changing all around me, and the people I grew up with were now growing apart.

I had started to meet many new people in high school. Some of those people were bad, and some were good. Yet once again I tried to fit in. I started cutting school, and that created more problems than it was worth.

I also got into a lot of trouble with my parents. My grades started to drop dramatically. You see, acting out, being disrespectful, and disregarding instructions can cause so much pain and suffering in your life.

In my first year of high school I met a guy named Lee. I fell head over heels in love with him. He played football and was super popular. He would occasionally walk me to school, and we would talk about whatever came to mind.

I was so in love with Lee, and I truly thought he felt the same about me. I was so sure that I gave him my virginity at the tender age of fourteen. Unbeknownst to me, that would be the beginning of many problems.

After giving my virtue to that boy who I thought loved me, I found out that was not the case. The reality was he didn't love me or want me. He only wanted sex from me. I was left hurt, neglected, unwanted, and taken advantage of.

Soon it began to feel like my mind and my life were all so distorted. One reason I felt that way was because people started to call me names like "whore." I started to hate school. I didn't want to go back. It became so bad that I started to act out. I cut school more often to hang out with my new friends. Back then I was just doing whatever without my parents even finding out.

One spring day I cut school with my friend Gina. We were hanging out at her house while her mother was gone. There were a couple of people in the front of the house. I didn't know them. That was my first time hanging out with Gina, and it was all new. A few of us kids were all hanging out in Gina's room. There was one guy named Herman. He sat on one bed. Gina and I sat on another. He flirted with me, and we talked a little. I didn't think he was cute, but I tried to be kind. Everything was okay at first, but things turned suddenly when I told him I wasn't interested. He changed. He suddenly started to have an attitude with me. I thought about leaving, but because I was at my friend's house and not at school, I stayed.

That was the worst mistake I could have made. He soon started threatening me. He started abusing me with words and objects. He threw pillows and small objects at me. He called me a b**** and other names.

Being young, insecure, and already set on a path of destruction, I started to really talk smack back to him, trying to defend myself. I talked about his looks. I talked about his clothing and everything. That got him very upset, and then all hell broke loose. The conversation just kept going back and forth until I had enough and walked out. But he wasn't finished . . .

I walked out the room and went into the bathroom because I had to use it. It was a tiny bathroom with a toilet, sink, and tub all squeezed together. Once in the bathroom I realized that my so-called friend's bathroom door didn't lock, so I held the door closed with my hand while I went. As I finished using the toilet I took my hand off the door while I pulled my pants up. Suddenly, the door opened, and Herman pushed his way in, knocking me off balance. I yelled at him and told him to GET OUT and LEAVE ME ALONE! I tried to push him to get him out the door. We began to wrestle in this tiny room. He shoved me onto the sink, then pushed me down onto the tub. I lost my balance because my pants weren't fully on. I hit my arms and back as I fell. I was trying to get away from him. I was yelling and screaming, telling him to stop. I started to feel trapped and felt like I couldn't breathe. I was yelling for my friend to help me while I kept fighting. It seemed like forever, but she finally came to the door. When she came in I thought he would leave me alone. But he turned around and yelled, "Get the f*** out of here!" And she turned and left.

I was like, "What!"

Gina just left me. I don't know if she was scared of him or what, but she left me. I felt betrayed. I kept asking myself why she would leave me there like that. I knew there were other people in the house, so I screamed. No one came to help me. I don't know if I had been set up or what, but there I was again, going back to my past abuse. Again I was wondering, "Why me?"

He continued to fight me, and I kept trying to fight back. I was crying and hurting from the pain of wrestling with him. I was scared and weak. Suddenly, I felt limp, but I kept screaming. He then put his hand over my mouth and pulled my underwear down. I was crying and got lost in my mind. I could not believe it. In that moment . . .

He raped me!

Just like that. It came out of nowhere. He got off me, pulled his pants up, and left the bathroom. I was stuck in an awkward position, halfway in and halfway out of the tub. I managed to get myself together just enough to get out the tub. I pulled my pants up, and I walked out of the bathroom. I don't remember seeing anyone. I didn't say a word. I just left the house. I ran home, but no one was there. I showered and cried, and I still didn't say a word when my parents came home.

I didn't tell anyone about that rape until Sunday morning at church. I became overwhelmed; I guess it showed on my face. A friend asked me, "What is wrong?" I was weighed down with what had happened, and I thought I could tell a friend at church what happened. I asked him not to say anything. But as soon as I told him, he told with a quickness.

I was sitting in Sunday school when my friend David, one of the pastor's sons who was like a brother to me, sat beside me. He asked me what was wrong. I was very down and out of it. I wasn't my normal self, and he knew it. I began to tell him what happened. When he left, he said he could not hold something like that. He said I needed to say something, and he went to get my parents.

We were in the hallway of the church when I told my parents what had happened. My father was upset, and my mother was stunned. We immediately left the church and went home. When we got there, my dad took off his church clothes and put on some loose-fitting clothes. I didn't know what was about to happen, but I knew it wasn't good. He told me to take him to where it happened. I tried to explain to my father that it happened at my so-called friend's house, but we went there anyway. My dad went to the door of that girl's house, but no one was there. Because we didn't know where the guy lived, we waited and waited for hours. My dad wanted to see this boy. I knew he wanted to put a hurting on him. No one came, so we finally left.

Joyce came down. We called the police, and I gave them all the information about what he had done. I also went to the hospital to get checked for rape. However, I had waited too long to say something; there was no evidence left on me. But the boy's history made it inevitable that he was going to serve time for what he had done to me. Come to find out while going through all that the boy had already been charged for similar attacks before mine.

I tried to erase that part of my life, but it kept rearing its ugly head. Sometimes when you try to forgive and leave the past in the past, the devil, our adversary, invokes our memory of those things and tries to make us feel like we are the victim all over again.

As I said, I was not the only person that man had raped. About three years ago, I was summoned to Las Vegas to testify about what he had done to me. He was on trial for raping and killing a woman. They wanted to put him away for good.

But I didn't have to go to Las Vegas; they had enough evidence to put him away without my testimony. He's currently in prison.

Those were some of the days of my youth. They would change me forever. All those life-changing events—bad, good, and indifferent—would contribute to the making of the woman I am today.

I wanted to do what I wanted to do, and it didn't get any better. I didn't feel any self-worth or personal value. I still tried to prove myself to people and fit in.

I started to develop depression and a lot of anger. I had to learn the hard way from middle school through adulthood. And when I say learn the hard way, I mean I left the church totally for a time. I was around seventeen, and I felt I needed to experience the world outside the church.

Receive Ye The Holy Ghost

When I received the Holy Ghost things were truly different, it was not as it was before. There were times I had to learn the hard way when it came to worldly things that I thought were ok to do being saved.

But, I learned, and had to listen to the Holy Spirit speak to me and guide me through the storms and trials of life.

Life can be challenging especially when you lack in your prayer life (prayerlessness). How was I going to hear the Holy Spirit unless I communed with God? You will start to fall short in many ways and at any age when you let your flesh take over.

"But I keep under my body, and bring it into subjection: lest that by any means, when I have preached to others, I myself should be a castaway." – 1 Corinthians 9:27

#wrestlingwithflesh
#prayerisdailyvictory
#exhalefleshinhaleholyspirit

❖

When You Think You're Grown, You Get Baby Daddies

D uring my young adult years I started partying. I was choosing men carelessly, smoking marijuana, and drinking alcohol; I even tried to sell crack. I thought I knew what I was getting myself into, but I didn't. I can recall hearing this quote, and it holds true today: "*A child is a child when it's convenient, but they are adults when they want to do what they want to do.*" I definitely found this true for me. I thought I was an adult by partying when I wanted to, smoking weed, and even attempting to sell crack. Why would I do things like that? What made me think it was okay? As I started to see things more clearly, I understood that it was me trying to partake in the vices of getting money, clubbing, and drinking. I know now that was never the right way. I was a slang-talking, tough, funny person, a sister girl from around the way. I was the person people liked to be around.

I remember the first—and last—time I tried to sell crack. Someone I knew wanted to buy some. During the transaction, he knew I had it in my hand, so he knocked it out of my hand, popped it in his mouth, and ran. That was the first and only time I tried to sell crack. I did some dumb stuff. I had a bumpy ride. I did not yield, stop, or even pay attention to the dead end signs. I just kept moving as fast I could.

When I was around seventeen I met a man named Rex. He was twenty-four and fine! Rex was around 5'9 with a caramel complexion. He had light brown eyes, a thin-to-medium build, and naturally curly hair with waves. He was well dressed. I would talk to him periodically on the phone. I would also see him around my church. I said *around* the church, not *in* the church.

When I turned eighteen I got more serious with Rex. I still thought he was too old, but he had a way with words, and he was persistent while I was naïve. Not knowing the game, I fell for his line.

He knew what to say to make me believe that he cared for me and wanted to be with me. I told him many things about my life. I felt like I could confide in him because he was older. I soon found out that it was all a game to him. It didn't matter; it was too late for me to turn back because I had fallen in love, had sex, and became pregnant.

Yes, I was pregnant. I was so happy. I thought that because I was pregnant we would be together and live happily ever after. But that was a dream, not reality. I began to find out about all his other women because I would find him in bed with them. To top it off, he had gotten another young lady pregnant. Her baby was due only a month before mine. Wow!

That was both surreal and my reality. And if all of this was not enough, I also learned he was a crack addict. He'd been in and out of prison since he was sixteen. I didn't start to see any of that until I opened my eyes. But it was too late; I had really got myself into some turmoil. After my beloved son was born, Rex was paroled after serving six months on another drug charge.

For him to get out that time he had to be paroled to my home. I had to understand the rules and stipulations of him being paroled to my home, and after understanding what was expected I decided it was okay. I felt that my son needed his father in his life, but that turned out to be a bad idea. After he had been paroled to my home I went with Rex to meet his parole officer. During that meeting the officer decided to give me a full rap sheet on Rex.

Now when I tell you it was a full rap sheet, I mean it was over forty pages. All I could do was look down and shake my head. All Rex did was laugh and shake his head. He even asked the parole officer why he had shared the information with me. The parole officer told him that he felt I should know what I was getting myself into when it came to Rex. I felt embarrassed. I couldn't believe this man had such a long record of criminal activity, including the sale of drugs, theft, and fraud.

In addition to everything else, Rex was also a womanizer; my friend told me not to fool around with him, but I didn't listen. It was a shame to learn all that about him. I can say this about him: he never tried to make me do drugs or anything else, but the thought of him doing things like that was sick. He claimed he wanted to change, but that change never came. I tried to pray for him; I even asked my parents and other family members to pray for him. One thing I do know is if the person doesn't want to change, that change won't happen. You have to want it, and he didn't want it.

We tried to make it work, but because I wasn't like the other girls he dated or the girls he played head games with, it wasn't going to work for us; I had my boundaries. I was subborn at times, and one good thing about all of that was that I knew God. Even in the midst of my many challenges and the stupid decisions I made as a young woman sinning in the world, I still got on my knees and prayed. I knew who I could turn to in times of trouble.

After hearing all of his indiscretions from the parole officer, my whole perception of Rex changed. It wasn't going down any longer. I was no longer willing to put up with him. Rex was going to have to be clean if he was going to be in a relationship with me. Rex had some respect, but he didn't have enough to stop using drugs or fooling with women behind my back. Sooner rather than later, he had to get out of my home, and it took me less than two months to realize that. He started smoking, drinking, and womanizing again, doing the same ole same ole.

However, I knew I had a son to take care of, and I wasn't going to subject him to the kind of lifestyle that would cause him to end up like his father. That curse was about to be broken.

I tell you that I put myself through a lot of messes, and it didn't have to be that way. I had to make my way back to my first love, Jesus Christ. I needed to do that, but I took my time and moved in my own direction. I hit more bumps and holes along the way.

Four years later I had another beautiful baby boy by another man named Chris. He was light skinned with long hair and wore glasses. He was around 5'8" with a medium build, and he was quite handsome. The interesting thing was that Chris was pretty much the same as Rex. He had gone to jail at a young age and, as he got older he was in and out of prison for drugs. And yes, he loved the ladies, and they loved him too. Chris was energetic, outgoing, and affectionate. He was fun at times. He liked going on outings to the beach and the park.

Chris and I had a longer relationship than Rex and I had. I thought I was in love with him, and that was truly blinding. At one time we actually were going to get married. At the beginning of our relationship, he was always around. He was trying to show me that he cared in many ways. He cleaned, cooked, and helped in any way he could, except financially. He could not get a job because he was fresh out of jail, so the financial burden fell on me. But things changed quickly; he was not the person I thought he was.

Chris and I had an on-and-off relationship for about three years. He felt I was the cause of our break up, but of course he would. When a man is doing wrong himself, he blames the woman. Our relationship was a constant struggle; he didn't like my eldest son's father. They argued about who was a better father, but neither one of them was really any good. Chris and I partied together at times, and he met a lot of my friends.

I recall a time when my girlfriend and I went out to a club. She stayed with me for a little while. On that particular night we came home around 1:30 a.m. I went into my room and went to bed. She slept on my sofa. In the middle of the night for no reason at all I woke up and went into the living room. When I got out there I saw Chris lying on the floor by the sofa. My friend was lying on the sofa. Her breast was hanging out of her blouse. When I saw Chris lying there beside her on the floor, I knew that something sexual had happened. When I woke them up, they both tried to deny that anything had happened. However, I was eventually told the truth. They both admitted that he had tried something sexual with her.

He was low down, dirty, and disrespectful. I found out later that Chris had sex with some of my other so-called friends and acquaintances. It was especially hurtful to think he was disloyal to me, the mother of his son. I don't know why I stayed with him so long.

While we were together Chris also started using drugs and became an alcoholic. There were also times when he was physically and verbally abusive to me. I remember one time when Chris and I were arguing in the car in front of my children. I was driving us to the house, and he reached over and started choking me. My children and I were scared. I could hardly breathe or say anything. My son yelled, "Leave Mommy alone! STOP!" I managed to slam on the brakes and tried to fight back. I know that incident affected my children; my oldest son remembers it to this day.

Chris and I didn't officially break up until I decided I wanted more for my life. He ended up going to prison for a long time for his many issues. We were together when he went in, but it was during that time I changed and ended our relationship.

While he was behind bars I was finally able to heal from past hurts and move on. When I finally moved on with my life mentally and physically, I was able to see clearly. It was then that I found the man I needed in my life.

❖

Abusive Attraction

Abuse is wrong on so many levels. I just want to state that information upfront. If you or anyone you know is going through abuse, you don't have to go through it, and you're not alone. There is a way to escape abuse: you have to move when God makes a way out for you.

This brings me to another extremely abusive relationship that I had. I want to make sure to tell you about this one because I am at a point where God has truly brought me out, and I want to testify about it.

My last abusive relationship was so bad that I can't even believe it happened to me. I met and started dating a man named TJ. He came into my life after I had my first child. He was after Rex and before Chris. TJ and I met through a mutual friend. He was doing a couple of months in the county facility, and I decided to talk to him. I asked myself why I was so attracted to jailbirds. However, the answer to that question is a whole other story.

TJ was dark skinned and around six feet tall. He had a lot of tattoos and was involved in gangs. He seemed nice at first, but as time went on I saw who he truly was. After dating this man for around six months, he claimed that he loved me. I came to find out that he loved me all right, and he showed me through his actions.

TJ loved me so much that he pulled a gun on me, not once but twice. The first time was after a party at his friend's house. That day we went to the home of his friend John and his wife's for a BBQ. We were all having a good time, and I told one of TJ's friends that he had pretty eyes. TJ felt I disrespected him by complimenting his friend. He was heated, and then he went crazy. He yelled and cursed at me in front of the other people at the BBQ. Everyone felt uncomfortable and got quiet for the rest of the day. I could hear some of the guests laughing and making jokes about it, but for the most part I got a lot of sad looks.

When we got home I thought everything was finished. Then out of nowhere he came into the livingroom very angry. He pulled out a revolver, put it to my head, and said, "Say goodbye to your son." This man showed a terrifying side of himself. In addition to that madness he would drink and get high on crack. He was truly crazy.

I got a little bold the second time he pulled a gun on me and said, "Well, if you're gonna shoot me, then shoot me." He didn't know that

I had already checked the gun and knew there were no bullets in it. However, he did pull the trigger, which showed his mindset. He could have slipped a bullet into the gun at any time and shot me. But thank God he didn't, and I'm alive today to tell about it.

There came a point when I was tired of TJ tormenting me. He was always fighting me and acting like a fool. I finally got a break when he ended up in jail again for a parole violation. During that time I was able to move into a two-bedroom apartment that was away from the four-bedroom place I had before. In my new place I was finally able to move on. I was getting some peace and, most important, I was getting some perspective.

On one of those peaceful days someone knocked on my door. It was TJ. I was shocked. Someone in my complex had told him where I had moved. Oh, my goodness, I couldn't believe it. When I opened the door and saw TJ, I almost lost my mind.

Immediately I knew I shouldn't have opened the door. But I did, and he wanted to come in. I was afraid to let him in, but I was more afraid of what would happen if I didn't.

Once inside he apologized for what he had done to me. There were no apologies that he could have given me that would change anything. I just wanted him out. No matter what he said, I just continued to suggest that he leave. When he saw that I didn't accept or want his apologies, he started to become aggressive. He really wanted me back, but I was not going to go back. When I refused him, he pushed me down. I fell into a round glass coffee table in my living room, and it broke. I was able to get up though.

I yelled at him, "You need to leave now, or I'm going to call my father!"

He said, "Call your daddy."

He wanted me to bring my dad into the situation. I decided to call the police instead. While I was on the phone reporting what he had done, he punched me in my face. He was laughing the entire time. I told the dispatcher that he had just punched me in the face. Suddenly, I looked to see my son standing there.

After hearing the sirens, TJ ran. I never saw him again. I last heard about him over fifteen years ago. I heard that he ended up serving life in prison for a murder he committed as a teen. (You shall reap what you sow.)

I never understood why I kept getting myself into these dilemmas. I allowed myself to go through so much stuff when I didn't have to. I thank God for His grace and mercy, giving me the ability to leave TJ when I did. But in all honesty, it was not easy by any means. I tried to find love and didn't even realize that I had it within me. I had to learn that for myself.

My mother would always tell me that I was looking for love in all the wrong places, like in that old country song. She was so right. Like I said before, I really needed to find my way back to my first love—the Lord and the church. I had some soul searching to do, and things had to change.

Over the course of my life I've had many difficult trials. Some of those trials were because of my bad decisions.

"(2) Arise, and go down to the potter's house, and there I will cause thee to hear my words. (3) Then I went down to the potter's house, and, behold, he wrought a work on the wheels. (4) And the vessel that he made of clay was marred in the hand of the potter: so he made it again another vessel, as seemed good to the potter to make it. (5) Then the word of the Lord came to me, saying, (6) O house of Israel, cannot I do with you as this potter? Saith the Lord. Behold, as the clay is in the potter's hand, so are ye in mine hand, O house of Israel." – Jeremiah 18:1-6

I needed a change in my life, and it was going to start with me. The men I had dated and had different relationships with during those times were toxic. I had to look at myself and ask, "God, what am I to do?" He was my potter. I needed him to make me over, to mold me into a woman that would wait on him. I felt like I let those forms of abuse take hold of me. I wasn't looking for those problems, but I invited them in. Because of that, the abuse only got worse.

I should have known better than to get myself into those situations, but it was too late. The enemy of God came to steal, kill, and destroy me, but Christ came so I could have life to the fullest.

Looking at it that way let me know that those circumstances had made me stronger. Those men took my heart, my self-worth, my whole outlook on men and molded them into a destructive force. They tried to destroy what God wanted for me. I had almost begun to feel like all men were mean, abusive, no-good, dirty dogs. I thought there couldn't be anyone else like the man who raised my sister and me. He loved my mother, and he loved and raised us as if we were his own children. Not only that, he showed us what we should expect from a real man—love, respect, protection, and communication—but none of that had come into my life. My dad Dennis, an upright man, was the only reason I thought a good man might exist.

Some of you may have experienced the same sort of abuse I have discussed in this chapter. You might even be discouraged. I, too, was a broken vessel that nobody thought was any good. Then Jesus picked up the broken pieces of my heart and revived it. He changed my heart, my worth, and my outlook on men. He also revived my soul.

I declare and decree healing in your life and deliverance.

You will not live in your past. You will have a life full of joy, peace, and love because you deserve it. You will not die, but live, and I will proclaim what the LORD has done (Psalms 119:17).

You are special. You are worth it. You will be okay.

#troubledontlastalways

"And after you have suffered a little while, the God of all grace {Who imparts all blessing and favor}, Who has called you to His {Own} eternal glory in Christ Jesus, will Himself complete and make you what you ought to be, establish and ground you securely, and strengthen, and settle you." – 1 Peter 5:10

SECTION 3

❖

IN THE MIDST OF IT ALL… I FOUND ME

CHAP TER ELEVEN

❖

#MommaMarilynMoment

I know there are many young women and men out there who really want to live fully for the Lord. They might be confused and struggling. We saints of God need to be honest with them and teach them the Scripture because the Word of God has the power to set them free.

Young people need consistency, activities, and renewal all of the time nowadays. They lose focus quickly. When no one is there guiding them or keeping up with them, they tend to drift quickly.

I know that because I was that young person who went astray. The enemy has new tactics to sway today's young people. We, as the body of Christ, must always stay fresh and consistent in our daily walk. That allows us to be examples and reflections of Christ.

We have to remind others and ourselves we are different. We must show that we are a chosen people. We are not a part of the world. We are special and appointed by God.

"And be not conformed to this world: but be ye transformed by the renewing of your mind, that ye may prove what is that good, and acceptable, and perfect, will of God." – Romans 12:2

Yes, looking at this we must know that we all have trials and tribulations. Nevertheless, we also have the strength to bear it and overcome it all through Christ. Amen.

❖

Be Still

My life today is so different from where it began. God has positioned me. He has given me a new life. All those things in the past are just that—in the past. I am active in my ministry and growing in Christ daily. God has blessed me with a life that I couldn't even imagine. I am walking in my destiny.

I am the mother of six children. I had two boys from my previous relationships. I also adopted three of my sister's children, two boys and a girl. My husband and I had one son together. I raised these six beautiful children with my loving husband Everett.

I would like to tell you our story. It is the story of how God blessed me with my husband. I met him about twenty-four years ago. We were at a social event. When I saw him, I knew immediately that I wanted to meet him. Everett stood around 5'6". He was handsome with a caramel skin complexion and a muscular build. He was such a gentleman. We exchanged numbers that night, and the rest was history.

Our relationship began as a strong friendship. We were friends before we got into a serious relationship. During that time I found out what a true man he was. He was faithful, loyal, and honest. Our love has stayed strong, and our relationship, marriage, and lives have only grown over time.

When Everett and I got together I had four children and adopted one more, but he didn't run away. As a matter of fact, he was especially considerate of my children; he never came over late, and he respected our house. He was always bearing gifts for my boys and me.

For years he would even come to my apartment for my children's birthday parties and bring them gifts. When he took me out to dinner or lunch, we would have serious conversations. I loved how he treated me like a lady. He opened the door for me and made sure I sat before he would sit. He was just a gentleman. It was different and just what I needed.

I remember when I had issues with my sons' father, he would listen to me vent and cry. He was there for me in the best way he could without interfering. He was such a good friend. We would eventually become more than that.

In 2002 we started to get more serious about each other. He had taken me out to eat, then he took me to a nice little spa. It was just him and me sitting there with soft music playing in the background. I was a little nervous because I didn't really know what was happening. I remember having butterflies in my stomach when he came close to me and said, "Marilyn, you're a good woman. I see you working hard trying to raise your children and your sister's children. I see all you do. I want to be in a more serious relationship with you and help you raise your children because I love you."

I thought that he was going to propose, but it wasn't time. However, it was time for us to be in a more committed relationship. We moved in with each other. During that time I became pregnant with our son. After our baby boy was born, we soon married.

I was still not in church when all of this happened, but that soon changed because I knew what God was doing in my life. I wanted to be in his will. So right before getting married, I started going back to church and reclaimed my salvation. From that day on, my life has been changed. My life was never the same from that moment on. God sent me a husband into my life. He was just what I needed. God blessed me with a good man, and yes, God blessed him with a good wife. Proverbs 18:22 says, "*He that finds a wife finds a good thing, and obtains favor from **The Lord**.*"

Everett came into our lives and became the husband I needed and the father my children needed. I no longer had to do things on my own. God heard my prayer.

My husband and I had many challenges. There was the death of my grandmothers, the death of his father, my cancerous thyroid issue, and his sarcoidosis. I could go on and on, but I'm here to tell you we made it and will continue through Jesus Christ.

Today our children are grown, with the exception of our baby boy. Our oldest son is married, and our other children are in school, working, and doing what they need to do as adults. I'm proud of them, and I thank God for his love and kindness toward my family.

When I look back over my life I can say that I am truly blessed, and I have to testify about it. I thank God for my wonderful husband. He has taken on roles that I could never handle and held me down in many areas of my life. There were times when I felt like breaking down, but my husband raised me up. It is a blessing to have him.

What We Needed

When you came into my life, you were just what I needed.

When you loved me the way you loved me, it was just what I needed.

When you held me in times of pain, it was just what I needed.

How can I repay you for giving me what I needed? That was by giving you what you needed.

It wasn't just about me, but it was also about you, and I realized that you needed me too.

You said to me, I was just what you needed.

The love I gave you, you said it was what you needed.

When you needed me in times of pain, you said to me I was just what you needed.

It wasn't about repaying, it was just about us, building our lives together and building trust.

We are one; God has blessed this Union.

I became a reflection of you, and you a reflection of me; we became a reflection of Christ.

And that's all we ever needed.

#Facebookministry

Just the other day I saw a young lady on Facebook that I've known throughout my life. She posted, "Feeling a bit discouraged today. When am I ever going to meet my (KING)? So ready to be in love like I love my God." I left her with Habakkuk 2:3 that says,

"For the vision is yet for an appointed time, but at the end it shall speak, and not lie: though it tarry, wait for it; because it will surely come, it will not tarry."

I want to encourage you to wait on God. Waiting on God is not always easy. Sometimes we want to use God like a microwave. A microwave is a fast way to cook things, to get something done. God does not work like a microwave. He uses the crockpot to cook things slowly. God also likes to work in things that are dried up. I remember the story I read in the Book of Ezekiel, where God looked at the dry bones and asked Ezekiel, "Can these bones live?" Ezekiel said, "Lord, thy knoweth," and the bones came together.

I decree and declare and that you will live and declare the works of the Lord. God works best when things aren't the way we would want them to be. When I was at the point of giving up, God sent me a mate to help raise my children and get my life together because I was a mess.

When I look back I see how many times I should have lost my life. I should have thrown in the towel. I should have given up, but I am glad that I am still standing. I want to encourage someone with these words. If you have experienced similar situations to mine, always remember when you feel you have no help, *"I will lift up mine eyes unto the hills from which cometh my help, my help cometh from the Lord . ."* (Psalms 121:1). Everything that we need comes from the Lord.

God is there always. He knows what we face in life every day. He promised to never leave us nor forsake us. I am standing on that promise. Jesus said in Matthew 28:20, *"Lo, I am with you always even until the end of the world."* We no longer can be bound by Satan because we have been set free by Christ. When he died on the cross, he set us free from all our problems, all our troubles, all our heartaches, all the things we suffer from when he said, *"It is finished."* I want to encourage you today to know that God is on your side. I'm a living witness of someone who knows what God can do, how he can make ways, and how he can turn things around. Just believe in him.

This is the last thing I leave you with:

"Beloved think it not strange concerning the fiery trials which come to try us some strange things happening to you but rejoice as much as he are partakers of Christ's suffering after this glory Shall be reveal ye shall be glad with exceeding joy." – 1 Peter 4:12

Every difficulty that I went through was a stepping stone toward higher ground in Christ. Continue to stand and walk in the holiness of

God. It may not always be easy, **but stand. BE STILL!**

"Stand fast therefore in the liberty wherewith Christ hath made us free, and be not entangled again with the yoke of bondage." – Galatians 5:1.

Family Testimonies

❖

My God Is Good. My God is Great.

For a while it seemed like something happened with our family every spring. In 2012 my father-in-law, who I loved dearly, passed away. It was a blow to our family, especially to my husband, but we got through it.

My Little Sis in the ER

In spring 2013 I got a call from a hospital asking me if I knew someone named E. When I said that she was my sister, I immediately asked what was wrong. They would not discuss it over the phone, but they asked if I could come to the hospital ASAP.

When I arrived at the hospital my sister was lying in the ICU on life support. She had tubes coming from her head that were draining blood. The doctors told me that when they finally found out who she was, my name and number came up as last known emergency contact.

"Wow!" I thought.

I started to weep so much. My sister and I had a broken relationship.

We hadn't talked in a while, and she hadn't spoken to her children. She was in a relationship that kept her away from us, but we prayed for her restoration. And there I was in this hospital as she struggled for her life in the ICU. I thought we were going to lose the opportunity to heal our relationship. I was distraught by the thought of it.

Then I heard the Lord's voice say, "Marilyn, do you trust me?"

I answered, "Yes, Lord, I trust you."

I found out that my sister had been in a car accident. I never found out the full details, but I do know that it almost killed her.

I decided to stay at that hospital day in and day out. I wanted to make sure people knew she had a family that cared about her. I was there to advocate for her and to make sure the doctors were doing what needed to be done. I also called on the prayer warriors.

When my mother got to the hospital she said, "Merl, the Lord promised me many years ago that He would not take her before she is born again."

My sister made it back from death's door. I believed in and trusted God. I also agreed with my mother in believing that God would save her before she left this world. Unfortunately, my sister still struggles with alcohol addiction and the trauma from the accident that put her in the hospital. I will continue to pray for her deliverance.

> *"Trust in the LORD with all your heart; and lean not unto your own understanding. In all your ways acknowledge him, and he shall direct your paths." – Proverbs 3:5-6*

#Trusting

When you trust God, you have direction. When you don't, you get lost.

How do you trust God? Know that He is and have FAITH!

The Loss of My Beloved Grammie Betty

In 2011 my Grammie Betty fell ill around my birthday. She was watching her favorite grandson, my son Roni. While on vacation I would call often to see how they were doing. One day I called, but that particular call didn't sound right. Grammie Betty told me she hadn't had a bowel movement, and she needed to go to the hospital. I told her we would come home right away.

We returned home and took her to the hospital. When we got there we found out she hadn't had a bowel movement in over three weeks. To make matters much worse, she had stage IV colon cancer.

My grandmother quickly began to lose hope when she had to undergo surgeries and many changes in her body. The doctors had to cut things out of her, which was hard to deal with and made her feel uneasy. She had to wear a colostomy bag, and the life she had known was no more. She became depressed and wanted to give up on life. However, she had a praying granddaughter and a family that loved her that wasn't going to give up on her.

I had to let her know that even though she was facing a challenge, God did not bring her that far only to abandon her. My Grammie Betty was a busy woman, doing many good things such as being a community activist, a daycare provider, and a family provider as well as fighting for the rights of children and teachers. She was dedicated to the betterment of her community, and I admired her for that.

During my Grammie's struggles with colon cancer I witnessed to her about God. That activated her belief and trust in God. Just like she had done for me, I was there for Grammie. I was there for every step of her illness. I cared for her the best way I knew how. In the midst of it all I prayed and I cried. I asked the Lord to heal her to keep her with us longer. I heard the Lord say, "Marilyn, do you trust me?" Then I heard Him say it again, so I replied softly, "Yes, Lord, I trust you." The doctor told us Grammie Betty had only three months to live, but we prayed so much that three months turned into almost a year.

I trusted God. I asked Him not to take my grandmother until she knew him as her Lord and Savior, until she was ready. I'm here to tell you that is what He did. The Lord used me to witness to my grandmother. I read the word of God to her every night, and she then became a member of our church. She received Christ into her life.

My Grammie started to fight and was feeling life, even in the midst of her sickness. Then when she became tired of fighting, the Lord took her home. The day before Grammie passed, she told the family to gather around her bed. She told us that she was tired and ready to be with the Lord. Later that same night, the Lord took her home. She was at peace.

That process was hard for me. It was the first time I had experienced a death of someone so close to me as a grown woman in Christ. But my sorrow became joy because I knew she was with the Lord. I still weep for my Grammie because I miss her presence, but I know all is well.

In 2 Corinthians 5:8 it says, "We are confident, I say, and willing rather to be absent from the body, and to be present with the Lord."

Renewed

Today, God has blessed me as I have endured. God helped me escape the bondage that the enemy sought to put upon me. Praise God! I had to be still, listen to God, and allow his light to shine through to me in times of darkness . . .

"Be Still, and know that I am God: I will be exalted among the heathen, I will be exalted in the earth." – Psalms 46:10

An Exhortation

❖

Let the Lord Use You

Whether you're young or old, we will go through troubles as saints of God. The devil has no respect for you as a person. I'm here to encourage you to lift your arms and never give up. We are just sojourners passing through this world. We have the power to overcome many obstacles that we will face in our lives.

Trust, Trust, Trust. Believe, Believe, Believe. Keep the faith and know that God will—I said God *will*—bring you out. I don't care what you may have gone through or what you're facing right now. You will make it. I said, YOU WILL MAKE IT! There is power in the tongue, and I'm here to speak life unto you. Live my sister! Live my brother! Don't let past or present circumstances oppress or overtake you.

When you were born God knew you were special, and so did the enemy. The enemy had a plan to destroy you. But God had a plan to restore you through Christ Jesus. Let's praise Him for restoration! Let's keep it moving.

#Letsgetit

#keepitmovin

#dontstopletsgetit

#weshallwearacrown

Prayer for Salvation

❖

Lord Jesus, come into my life, save me, and cleanse me of all my sins. I am a sinner and need to be made whole. Take away my pain, take away my past, cleanse me with your blood, and make me whole. I confess with my mouth that you are my savior, the true and living God. I believe in my heart that God raised you up from the dead, so I will and shall be saved.

Father God, in Jesus' name I repent of all my sins and open my heart for Jesus to reign inside me. Jesus, you are my Lord and Savior. Fill me with your Holy Spirit, purge me of all my sins with your blood, and wash me white as snow. I want to be what you have called me to be. I want to stand on your word and your promises. I thank you, Jesus, for saving me and sending your spirit so that I will have a comforter. Lord, fill my cup and let it run over. In Jesus' name,

Amen.

Romans 10:9 says, "That if thou shalt confess with thy mouth the Lord Jesus, and shalt believe in thine heart that God hath raised him from the dead, thou shalt be saved."

#Ihaveconfessed

Luke 15:10 says, "Likewise, I say unto you, there is joy in the presence of the angels of God over one sinner that repenteth."

#Angelsrejoice

#IamSAVED

About the Author

❖

A s a licensed childcare provider and a sought-after coach and Mentor to business owners and families seeking the best for their children, Marilyn Randolph has shaped the course of countless lives.

Randolph has impeccable professional credentials. Having earned an BS degree in Human Services and AA in Social Behavior with an emphasis in Business and Early Childhood Education along with permits from the State of California, she is well prepared to meet the challenges presented by developing children. Seeking to extend her community outreach, she started the Betty Howard Memorial Scholarship Fund to help students in early childhood education by offering funding at the junior college level. A mer-it award of $250 is annually bestowed to the winner of the scholarship. Along with those efforts she oversees the distribution of gifts to over one hundred children in the community every Christmas and has been delivering such joy over the past twenty years. She is also Founder and Executive Director of Women Rising Above Abuse (WRAA) that started in 2017. March 14th 2019, she was appointed and is now serving as Commissioner of Human Rights of the Santa Clara County.

Marilyn Randolph is also a licensed Evangelist and Minister of Kingdom Worship Center International of San Jose. Randolph finds her inner direction in the grounding of her faith. To those clerically involved roles she also has contributed as purity president, locally and District wide, Board of Trustees, Youth Department Chairwomen, and Junior Church mother assistant.

Family is at the core of her beliefs and values. She is married with six children, three of whom are adopted, and a grand daughter.

Randolph is a noted author, having written *Be Still*, a volume that will be published in 2016 and Brighter Beginnings Family Child care guide that explores the subject of opening a business in FCC. She is also a publisher and Coach to those that want to be and has become, Authors . Future plans include continuing to travel to minister, building her successful consulting business, and supporting scholarships on an ongoing basis to continuing students in early child-hood education at the junior college level in California.

Self-Love

Nourish, Cherish, Protect

Devotional Journal

When writing anything, it's sometimes hard to know where to start but, I tell those that have asked me how I started, to begin by writing." That's precisely what I was doing when I began this Self-Love Journal.

This Journal may be a little different than an average journal and different than what I have ever done before.

I am a dual author, and I've written two books one about my transformation, "Be Still" the other is a guide to help to start a business in the field of Family Child Care "Brighter Beginnings Family Child Care Guide." However, I have now created this to help you on your journey to Self-Love.

I had to pray and ask God what I should write in this Self-Love Journal that would help someone reading it learn how to love themselves.

This will be your Journal journey book to learning how to Self-Love. Self-Love is a powerful thing, and some people may feel that it is putting yourself before God, but, it's just the opposite. The Love of Christ is in us, so we must love ourselves and others. If you don't love yourself, then how could you love anyone else?

Ephesians 5:29-30 (AMP)

For no one ever hated his own body, but {instead} he nourishes and protects and cherishes it, just as Christ does the church because we are members {parts} of His body.

You see, you must love yourself, and there are steps to do this. Therefore, I would like to share with you what I have learned, and then you can also share and take notes. Write in your journal, create your story or journey to Self-Love Through Christ. You never know, it can one day become a book if you choose to become an author or you can have it for yourself to reflect and look back on.

I pray this journal helps you develop that Self-Love within yourself. I want you to know that I love you, but most of all you are loved by the Most High God & our Savior Jesus Christ...

Nourishment...

The food or other substances necessary for growth, health, and good condition.

Naturally

When most people wake up in the morning, what do we do? We eat breakfast, but what kind of breakfast does one eat? Either it will be healthy or unhealthy. If you eat unhealthy food it may cause some health issues within your body such as diabetes, or high blood pressure, etc. However, if you smoke a substance like cigarettes or marijuana, it may cause asthma or some form of cancer.

Anything that you inhale into your lungs may cause various health problems; it's just what it is. I remember years ago when I was a young woman in my early 20s, I would smoke cigarettes and drink coffee for breakfast. So unhealthy and I knew it, but I did it anyway. Then when I did eat breakfast, I would fry my pancakes in a little vegetable oil with extra syrup and butter. This was so bad. I knew it was, but I still did it, I developed asthma, cancerous thyroid issues, and had nodules growing around my thyroid which ended up with me having surgery and getting it removed. It was terrible. Not only did I have that issue, but I had also developed high blood pressure. Now, some may say that my thyroid issues could not be from smoking, but what I read on WebMD it noted that "women who smoked were twice to develop overactive thyroid caused by Graves' disease." I knew this before I even read it. I was a chain smoker and reading on the box of my carton or pack, it stated that it might cause cancer. When they told me that my thyroid was cancerous, I knew it was because of those cancer sticks I smoked.

Spiritually

When you wake up in the morning, what should we do? Prayer, devotion, study the word of God (Holy Bible). If we don't pray and have that time with our Father, what happens is that we do not get our nourishment for the day and things will begin to be unbalanced. It's like we skip a meal, and now you have opened the door for the enemy to make us sick.

People start to get on our nerves quickly, and things start to happen that we did not notice coming our way. We don't see as clearly as we would if we nourish our spirit as we should daily. Now, I'm only speaking of experience because, when I didn't pray and have that time with my Father God, I started to notice the attacks of the enemy and how it started to affect me. I remember a time when being financially overwhelmed, my payments were late from clients and agencies, my husband and I began to argue, my children arguing about really nothing, and it was just straight chaos in the house. I needed to get back to what nourished my spirit. Time with God is so essential, if you don't have that nourishment with our Father God, you leave room for the attacks of the enemy. When you feed yourself right, you will grow and become stronger and healthier, and you can resist the enemy and his devices.

Let Him nourish you!

How will you start to nourish your mind, body, and soul?

_____

_____

_____

_____

_____

_____

_____

_____

_____

_____

_____

_____

_____

_____

Protection

The action of protecting someone or something, or the state of being protected. A person or thing that prevents someone or something from suffering harm or injury.

Naturally

I have children, and some of you may be able to relate when it comes to protecting our children. Because of my past abuse, I wrote about in my book "Be Still" if you haven't read it, please get it. Anyway, because of my past abuse, I was very protective of my children and always made sure they were safe. Some may have felt I was too protective, but I didn't care; they were my children, and I wanted to make sure that no hurt, harm, or danger came upon them.

When they were sick, I took them to the doctor. My grammie would get so frustrated with me that she would say "girl you always taking them children to the doctor, for every little thing" and yes, I did. Even when my oldest had to go to the restroom and have a bowel movement, I would pick him up from school to use the bathroom at my grandmothers. Since I worked there, it was around the corner. Yes, maybe that was a little too much, but still, I felt I needed to care for them and protect them in every way possible.

Spiritually

When I talk about spiritual protection, this is far greater than natural because our Father God is our Jehovah Sabaoth, our protector. He protects us from things seen and unseen, naturally and supernaturally. I recall this time while driving in the car and feeling defeated and felt the weight on my back; it was so heavy, the only way I can describe the pressure would be like I was carrying tons of bricks on my back. I ended up having to stop at the gas station to put gas in my car; I was so engulfed in thought regarding my son that I wasn't even paying attention and turned the car on with the gas nozzle still pumping gas and drove off. My God! I tell you I could have blown up BUT GOD! When I tell you God protected me, Whooh! I will never forget that day! There is a gospel song by Kirk Carr I love and it's called, God Blocked It, He wouldn't let it be so.

Let Him be your Jehovah Sabaoth.

How will you protect your mind, body, and soul?

_____

_____

_____

_____

_____

_____

_____

_____

_____

_____

_____

_____

_____

_____

_____

_____

Cherish

Protect and care for (someone) lovingly. Hold (something) dear. Keep (a hope or ambition) in one's mind.

Naturally

I have had many women in my life that has planted in me, and I cherish every one of those women. I hold them dear to my heart. My mother, my cousin, who was a second mother to me, my maternal and fraternal grandmothers, my great grandmother and great aunt. These women showed me so much love and planted in me so many things that I cherish today. My fraternal grandmother taught me about entrepreneurship; she owned her own business and ran it until the day she passed. She was dedicated to her community and the children she was raising. Today I still run that business and pray that I will be able to one day open a pre-school in her name. I will forever protect and hold her dear legacy because of the woman she was and what she has done for me and so many during her lifetime.

Spiritually

My great aunt, mother, and cousin, who was like a mom to me, planted more of a spiritual seed in me. They taught me how to seek God, in prayer, praise, and worship. I remember as a child my great aunt would go to Noon Day prayer, I was little and didn't understand how it was so important to have that time with God but, as I grew, I learned how important it was and still is. During those adolescent years, I played in the pews and even fell asleep while the women of God whaled and prayed and sought God until His Holy Spirit came into the room. When the spirit of God came were having that intimate time with God. It is so powerful. I learned just how powerful it was at the age of 12 when God filled me with the His Holy Spirit. I couldn't stop praising God. He says in His word, ask and it shall be given, seek and you shall find, knock and the door shall be open. Matthew 7:7. I sought, and I received. Cherish your time with God....

How will you cherish your mind, body, and soul?

_____

_____

_____

_____

_____

_____

_____

_____

_____

_____

_____

_____

_____

_____

_____

_____

_____

Self-Love

I want to leave you with this. When it comes to loving you, you must be Mindful of who you are and don't worry about what others want you to be or even think you should be. God created you, and you are fearfully and wonderfully made Psalms 139:14. Know what you want, and move forward in it, stay focused on your goal. Love yourself enough to care for yourself as you would your child, husband, or parents. Protect yourself. Don't let people around you that mean you know good in your circle. You must set boundaries. Don't let anyone physically, spiritually, or emotionally affect you in a way that they have control. Know this and repeat after me.... You are special, you are worth it, and you will be okay. Now go! Walk in your calling with confidence.

Love,
Marilyn

**ARE YOU A SURVIVOR OF ABUSE,
DOMESTIC VIOLENCE OR HUMAN TRAFFICKING?**

The time you spend with God reflecting on the questions, testimonies and biblical truths in this workbook will lead to a miraculous healing and your complete restoration.

Though the pursuit of love promises to be difficult, there is one person worth fighting for and Jesus said it's YOU!

Order your copy today!
loveneverfai lsus.com/shop

MARILYN RANDOLPH

BE STILL: EXCERPT

"...That's when he pushed me down. I fell on her bed, and he hit me. Stunned, I had no idea what and why he was doing that. I said, "What are you doing?" I thought my voice would cause him to see me. He kept saying something, but I was so shocked by his hitting me that I couldn't understand what he was saying. It was like being under water..."

LOVE

JOY

Courage

BE STILL

Believe

Victory

Triumph

Strength

U.S. ABUSE STATISTICS

- Every 98 seconds an American is Sexually Assaulted
- 1 out of every 10 rape victims are male
- 82% of all juvenile victims are female

(Source: https://www.rainn.org/statistics/)

"I didn't know it at the time, but God was ordering my steps, even as a little girl. From that day forward I kept moving; I didn't let what that man did affect my footstep."
-Marilyn Randolph

#Thedevildidnothavehisvictory

BOOKING INFORMATION

Phone: 530-430-7743

Email:

marilynrandolph@marilynrandolph.com

Add it to the Library!

- BOOKSTORES
- COLLEGES & UNIVERSITIES DOMESTIC VIOLENCE ORGS
- COUNTY FAMILY SUPPORT CENTERS
- PUBLISHERS: Multi-book Author

Content advisory reader discretion chapter six

http://marilynrandolph.com

WHO WE ARE

WOMEN RISING ABOVE ABUSE IS A NONPROFIT COMMUNITY LOOKING TO HELP WOMEN OVERCOME ABUSE IN ALL FORMS.

MISSION

Our Mission at WRAA is to help women And girls who have suffered unresolved hurt and trauma caused by sexual, emotional, and physical abuse heal both spiritually and naturally. We provide a safe environment and help these women and girls move from a life of hopelessness to a life empowerment through Love. We want to give them tools necessary to succeed, and to move forward with a renewed spirit.

FORMS OF ABUSE
Emotional Abuse, Physical Abuse sexual Abuse

EMOTIONAL ABUSE

Happen when someone insults, humiliates or uses "to control another person. It can happen to people in all income, education, and ethnic groups.

Emotional Abuse doesn't always lead to physical violence however almost all physical or sexual abuse includes emotional abuse. Being emotionally abused puts a person at risk of physical abuse.

Emotional Abuse is Hard to Recognize
• The abused person may not ever realize it's happening
• This can make it hard to take steps to stop it
• The longer the abuse goes on, the more harmful it can be;

Women Rising Above Abuse

I'm not ashamed of my past.
The decisions
I made good or bad I own.
They made me the women I am
today. I may have fallen, but out
of those trials arose a STRONG,
CONFIDENT women
who knows who
She is. You cannot break me.
I will always rise above!

WOMEN RISING ABOVE ABUSE
3155 San Felipe Rd #97
San Jose, Ca 95135
email: info@womenrisingaboveabuse.org
phone: 493.589.8617

www.womenrisingaboveabuse.org

PHYSICAL ABUSE
Physical abuse is the most visible form of abuse and may be defined as any act that results in a non-accidental trauma or physical injury.

• The longer the abuse continues, the more serious the injuries to the person and the ore difficult it is to eliminate the abusive behavior:

SEXUAL ABUSE
Sexual abuse is any sort of non-consensual sexual contact. Sexual abuse by a partner/intimate can include derogatory name-calling, refusal to use contraception, deliberately causing unwanted physical pain during sex, deliberately passing on sexual diseases or infections and using objects, toys, or other items (e.g. baby oil or lubricants) without consent and to cause pain or humiliation.

CHILD SEXUAL ABUSE
• Sexual touching of any part of the body, clothed or undothed
• Penetrative sex, including penetration of the mouth
• Encouraging a child to engage in sexual activity including masturbation
• Intentionally engaging in sexual activity in front of a child
• Showing children pornography, or using children to create pornography
• Encouraging a child to engage in prostitution

How to get Help.
If you are a sexual abuse survivor, or you think you may have been a victim of sexual abuse, peer support can be very helpful. Remember that it was not your fault.

WOMEN RISING ABOVE ABUSE

Women Rising Above Abuse

BREAK
THE
SILENCE

WHY WOMEN RISING ABOVE ABUSE?

I started Women Rising Above Abuse because I know our community is need of it. As a child, I was molested and raped. During that time of my life I had no outlet, nor was there any program that we knew of that could help me through those trying times. I wanted to be delivered and healed from those past hurts, yet I found myself in emotionally and physically abusive relationships as time went on. Today, I am an overcomer, empowered, and strengthen. I am no longer a victim of my past hurts or traumas. I want to help young girls and women become overcomers themselves. This my calling and what I desire to do, in 1 Thessalonians 5:11 (KJV) it says; Therefore, encourage and comfort one another and build up one another, just as you are doing. We should not have to live our lives in fear or shame but, in peace and joy.

You are special, you are worth it, you will be okay

Marilyn Randolph
Executive Director

God is in the midst of her, she shall not be moved; God shall help her, just at the break of dawn:" Psalms 46:5 NKJV

Emotional Abuse: 1.800.621.HOPE (4673)
Sexual Abuse: 1.800.656.4673
Physical Abuse: 1.800.799.SAFE (7233)

COME SPEND AND HOUR IN THE

OVER*FLOW*

WHERE THE BLESSINGS DONT STOP!

MARYLIN RANDOLPH

LETITIA CAMPBELL

TUNE IN TO THIS EXCLUSIVE PODCAST CALLED "THE OVER FLOW".
FROM A PEN TO AN ANCHOR, JOIN US AS WE HAVE A CONVERSATION
ABOUT RELEVANT SUBJECTS OF OUR TIMES.

FOR MORE INFORMATION CALL:
(530) 430-7743

Your Encounter Awaits

Join us for one hour of intentional prayer every Tuesday @ 7:00 PM

The Godly Girls Network

Celebrating 17 Years of Impactfttl Ministry

www.godlygirlsnetwork.com

0 Facebook.com/GGNLady

234 E. Gish Road, Suite 300. San Jose, CA 95112
Overseer Rev. Donna Edward

HAVE YOU HEARD THE WORD?

THERE'S A NEW
CHURCH
IN TOWN BUILDING PEOPLE AND FAMILIES BY PROMOTING KINGDOM PURPOSE & BUSINESS

LEAD BY SENIOR PASTOR TERESA TATE

KINGDOM WORSHIP
CENTER INTERNATIONAL JOIN SUNDAY AT 10:30 AM & WEDNESDAY AT 7:00 PM

234 E. GISH ROAD, SUITE 300. SAN JOSE CA 95112

FACEBOOK.COM/KWCICHURCH

Made in the USA
Middletown, DE
06 May 2022

65353526R00086